My Oxford

Catherine Wesselinoff (nee Haines) is a teaching and research scholar in philosophy at the University of Notre Dame, Australia. She completed a Combined Honours Degree in English Literature and Philosophy at the Australian National University in 2009, a master's degree in English literature at the University of Oxford in 2012, and a PhD in Philosophy at the University of Sydney in 2022. She lives in Sydney with her husband and son.

My Oxford

Catherine Haines

PARTHIAN

Parthian, Cardigan SA43 1ED
www.parthianbooks.com
First published in 2019 by New Welsh Rarebyte
This edition published by Parthian in 2025

Print ISBN 978-1-917140-06-5
Ebook ISBN 978-1-917140-07-2
Editor: Gwen Davies
Typeset by Syncopated Pandemonium
Printed by 4edge
Published with the financial support of the Books Council of Wales
British Library Cataloguing in Publication Data
A cataloguing record for this book is available from the British Library.
Printed on FSC accredited paper

Dedicated, in memoriam,
to Howard Mak (1987–2009)

...We are oft to blame in this
'tis too much proved, – that with devotion's
visage,
and pious action we do sugar o'er
the devil himself.

William Shakespeare, *Hamlet*

What follows is, in its essence if not in its contours, a memoir about my experience with anorexia nervosa while I was a postgraduate student at the University of Oxford. My intention is not to contribute to the plethora of 'treatment texts' written by 'recovered' anorectics. (I am not 'recovered': I am 'recovering'). I would like to impart some information, ideas, and feelings about some aspects of my experience to others currently suffering from an eating disorder, directly or indirectly. I've chosen to narrate and reflect on the year I spent in Oxford because I would like to a) question whether a possible equation exists between my compulsion to starve and pressure to read and write and b) re-consider the religious conversion I underwent during that time.

1. Hong Kong

At the beginning of July 2011, I went on a diet.

It was the summer between my bachelor degree and graduate school. I was staying with my parents in their apartment in Hong Kong. I had gained weight, and felt that the most effective use of time would be to focus on losing it. My mother suggested the Cambridge Weight Plan, a programme which is based on the concept of meal replacements, sachets of minerals and nutrients, which contain 200 calories each and dissolve in water. Combining three of them a day with a meal of pure protein supposedly provides a balanced diet.

Cambridge works partly by pushing the body into a state of ketosis. Ketosis is a Greek word meaning 'sweet condition', and accounts for the 'high' that anorexics routinely cite. It is the consequence of a diet that is very low in carbohydrates. A body denied sugar enters a metabolic state, during which it is almost completely fueled by fat. These release 'ketones' into the blood stream. Ketones are the most addictive compound on earth. Just as a heroin addict chases substance-induced highs, anorexics depend on chemicals – our own. Anorexia strikes classically good girls in good families. Good girls are often people pleasers and perfectionists but we, too, can become drug addicts.

There was a lot of pre-reading for my course, and I was writing a novel, so I established a routine to facilitate these practices while I was fasting. By the end of August I had accomplished my academic, creative and weight-loss goals. To this day, I do not know why I failed to resume my (abnormal, bulimic, disordered) relationship with food. I simply continued to do what I had already been doing: every day, I restricted my nutritional intake to 1,000 calories or less. This continued throughout the months I was completing my Master's degree, so that by July 2012, I was very severely underweight and had been diagnosed with anorexia nervosa.

2. Michaelmas

The St Peter's College MCR (Middle Common Room) refers to two things: firstly the group of postgraduates within the College and secondly, the common room itself in which we socialised and worked. It was here during Noughth week (the week before term starts) that someone asked me: 'What are you writing your dissertation on?'

'The mind-body problem.'

'I thought you were studying English?'

'I'm interested in the overlap between philosophy and literature.'

'What text will you study?'

'*Hamlet*.'

'Then you can tell everyone what "to be or not to be" actually means.'

'Exactly.'

'What *does* it mean?'

'Is it better to be alive or not alive? Or rather, is it better to exist or not exist?'

'Life isn't that bad.'

'Death might be worse. It all depends on whether or not you believe in the immortality of the soul.'

'He's debating whether or not to kill himself, right?'

'That is how it is traditionally understood."

"Why does he want to kill himself?'

'That is the question.'

'Ah hunh. It's a cool topic... I'm getting hungry. Shall we go to dinner in hall?'

'Is it time?'

'Just about.'

'I'll head off, then. I've got some stuff to do back in my room. See you later.'

I walked out the back gate of the college, through the Castle Complex, onto Paradise Street, into the St Peter's Graduate Annexe, up the stairs, opened my door, lay on the bed, and fainted.

The following day I met my supervisor for the first time. I explained that even though I had but a cursory understanding of analytical philosophy, and had never studied theology, I wanted to a) define and contextualise the sixteenth-century model of the self and b) explain Shakespeare's position with regard to it. My supervisor explained that in order to fully appreciate Shakespeare, I had to understand every thinker preceding him. He suggested I start with Plato and go as far as Luther via Augustine and Aquinas before beginning to analyse *Hamlet*. Try and fit that in by Christmas while learning two ancient languages, sleeping five hours a day and living on 1000 calories. As I left my supervisor's study and walked towards the Bodleian, I resolved to drop my BMI to eighteen by Easter, just to see if I could. It was a matter of pure curiosity.

Each day, I wake at precisely 4am. Strip, go to the bathroom, step onto the scales. Breath. Make a cup of herbal tea, sit at the desk and take notes until 6am. Walk down Paradise Street to the gym. Run for 60mins, burn 500 calories. Return to the Annexe, shower, exfoliate, moisturise, dress. 9am. Make an omelette – two eggs, 70 calories each, 140 calories, plus cheese, 60 calories, 200 calories. 800 calories remaining. Walk to the library. Study....

Plato's conception of the mind-body problem says that the soul, caught in the 'grave of the body', is liberated through a weakening of precisely this body. Salvation occurs when the soul is set free from its prison-body. The soul is then free to live in the realm of pure forms, where it 'can behold the absolute Good.'

A bit dizzy? A throat lozenge? Step outside for a cigarette. Lip gloss *and* chewing gum? 11:30, go to

Pret a Manger. Buy 100 calories. Protein or green veg. Consume. 700 calories remaining. Return to the library. Study....

Plato's explanation impressed the hypersexual St Augustine of Hippo and the overweight Thomas Aquinas centuries later. In 1517, Luther also more-or-less agreed, saying, 'Man has a twofold nature, a spiritual one and a bodily one.'

2pm. Consume 200 calories. 500 calories remaining. Walk to class. Burn excess by walking fast. Speak. Listen. 4:30, go to Marks and Spencer and have another 100 calories. 400 calories remaining. Go to the MCR. Talk. Listen. Go back to the Annexe. Shower, change, email, go to dinner, at college or with friends. 400 calories of protein and greenery and alcohol included. 'End Game'. 10pm, go to bed. Sleep. And again.

For months, I closely studied medieval Christian thinkers, all of whom claimed that mind and matter are separate and ergo that the soul is a) immortal and b) damnable. By Easter I had lost so much weight that I had to wear four layers of clothes to stay warm. Dionysius was likewise driven mad by his education.

A growing body of research has focused on the relationship between the frequency with which women read and their potential anorexic risk. Mainly this work links the presence of eating-disordered thinking with women's reading of beauty and fashion magazines, rather than their reading of poetry and philosophy from Homer to Rousseau. But in any case, the notion of disordered reading suggests that certain subjects are inherently more open to being affected by text; that our boundaries are essentially more permeable, more receptive to the leaky toxicity of words. We are 'dupes' who consume too many unsound ideological representations.

3. Christmas and New Year

I spent the Christmas holidays with my extended family in Scotland. It was the ultimate nightmare. I hadn't been in a situation where I was 'required' to eat three meals a day for six months – I had certainly eaten no more than a single meal once or twice a week, in front of friends, for the duration of that time.

When I first arrived at my uncle's house, I tried to maintain my structured 'system' of 1,000 calories of pure protein a day, while appearing to eat 'normally'. Thus mealtimes brought tremendous stress, anxiety, and fear. I had to manage people and their perceptions in addition to my own willpower. Needless to say, everyone noticed and my eating habits were a hot topic of discussion, and so I ate more, in order to assuage their censure. Consequently, I experienced food as force. The guilt I felt when I 'overate' was enormous and I was desperate to find opportunities to make up for all the 'extra' calories I had consumed. I couldn't stop thinking about the food or tabulating what I'd eaten at the expense of enjoying myself and socialising. Just worrying about how to socially engineer the situation was exhausting.

For New Year's Eve, I travelled to Rome to celebrate with a friend from High School. This particular friend has seen me through every stage of my illness, by providing unconditional support and without expressing criticism. On that occasion, as she has on others, she succeeded in loosening me up. During our holiday, I ate gelato and drank champagne, I had pizza and pasta, and, at the time, I didn't feel guilty about it. That was the last time I ate by choice.

Our visit to the Vatican drove home for me the reality of a lot of the material I had been studying in theory and reading in isolation. My friend and I had a number of very serious religious discussions – she herself is a lapsed Catholic – as a result of which I actually considered Damnation for the first time in my life, and to accept damnation as a realistic possibility means to take on the hardest battle any human being can fight.

4. Hilary

When I returned to Oxford I had a conversation with a priest. I had been christened when I was a child, but I was deeply concerned about the state of my soul. I wanted to be confirmed and come into full communion with the Church. The priest said this would require a period of Catechumenate. He placed my name on the Rite of Election, and said that if he were convinced that I was ready to make a faith commitment to Jesus, I could receive the sacrament of the Holy Eucharist at Easter.

I observed Lent, which meant embracing my fast with a ferocity of newness, restricting further the amount and type of food I ate. Regarding it as the final period of purification and enlightenment, I promised myself – promised God – that I would begin to eat on Easter Sunday and enter the moment of Resurrection. I would be saved and my new life would begin.

I struggled to uphold my previous routine that term, because I was no longer able to eat even 1,000 calories, and the protein stuck in my throat. I had a violent, visceral reaction of nausea and repulsion – akin to an epileptic fit – whenever I saw food, and whenever I ate, I experienced extreme pain. Consequently, I felt always as though I were about to faint. The moment I began to carry on an extended conversation with anyone, even a shopkeeper or a librarian, I would see stars. I was unable to remember the start of my own sentences upon their completion. I could not hold several numbers, or several words, or several complex concepts simultaneously. I ceased connecting one thing to the next, ceased even feeling obliged to do so. I stayed in my room, wrapped up in blankets, in front of a blow heater, working with the text of *Hamlet* (Otherwise known as *Spectre Afoot*!).

Hamlet begins one night on the ramparts of Elsinore Castle, when Prince Hamlet encounters the ghost of his father, the late King. Prince Hamlet says:

Be thou a spirit of health or a goblin damned
Bring with thee airs from heaven or blasts from hell
Be thy intents wicked or charitable.

He doesn't ask, 'Are you real or not?' There can be no question. There is a ghost. The Elizabethan audience knew it. The ghost was real in their belief system. We know it too. It's in the list of characters and is listed as a speaker in the text. (We also know it's an actor. That is, it is both real and not real) So when the ghost tells Hamlet that his father was murdered by his uncle, the current king, Claudius, and demands that Hamlet avenge him, Hamlet agrees to do as instructed. Privately, however, Hamlet, remains uncertain of the ghost's veracity.

I closed the book. It was dinnertime and I'd promised a friend I'd meet him at the Turf Tavern. So I got dressed, wrapped myself in my coat, and headed for the door, just as I'd done countless times before, when a voice observed, 'You are leaving the room.'

I looked around and there was no one there. I walked on, down the stairs, across the hall when she spoke again.

'You are opening the door,' she said.

I stopped, and closed my eyes. My head spun. I stepped outside.

'You are walking along the street.'

I saw stars. I was worried I would collapse so I walked back towards my room very slowly. I paused outside the kitchen. Perhaps if I ate something....

'Do Not Eat,' said the voice.

I lay on my bed and closed my eyes. I started

replaying my own actions in my head while she commented on them. I had a sense of looking at myself through the critical eye of another, watching my own figure– my 'double' – viewing the scene from up above....

I woke up the next the morning and made an omelette for breakfast. As I lifted the fork to my mouth, the voice said, 'Do Not Eat!' and my wrist flicked, throwing it against the wall.

Frightened that I had some sort of involuntary muscular disease, I went to the doctor.

'What seems to be troubling you?'

'I haven't had a period for six months.'

'Is there any possibility you could be pregnant?'

'No.'

'Have you experienced tiredness?'

'Yes.'

'Lie on the bed.' He pressed into the lower part of my stomach with his fingers. When I sat up again, he listened to my chest, and then asked me to get on the scales.

'Have you noticed any weight loss?' he asked.

'Yes, I suppose so.'

'It's possible you have Crohn's disease, which is a chronic bowel disorder. Alternatively, this is a hormonal imbalance. We should run some tests.'

'Alright,' I said, standing up to leave. He looked at me.

'Sit down again for a moment please,' he said. 'There is a chance... do you think you might have an eating disorder?'

'No,' I said.

'Are your thoughts or behaviors around food or weight making it difficult for you to enjoy life?'

'No.'

'Alright. I'll book you in for an ultrasound. You can go now, go see the nurse for a blood test and urinary sample.'

I walked out the door and out of the clinic and never went back. It was extremely cold. I headed down Walton Street towards the Annexe. My hands were purple. I was light-headed: there was a party that night, so I was saving all my calories to have in front of friends. I decided to rest until it was time to get ready.

There was a knock on the door.

'Yes?'

'Are you OK?'

'Um, yeah, fine.'

'You didn't show up tonight or last night, and you're not answering your phone. Can I come in?'

'Just give me a sec.'

I pulled on my dressing gown and opened the door.

'You look awful,' he said.

I saw myself reflected in the glass window behind him. I was skeletal. My shoulders were hunched and my eyes were hooded. I looked like a Devil.

'It's just the flu.'

'Can I get you anything?'

'No, I'm fine thanks.'

'Ok. Well, let me know if there is anything I can do....'

'I'll let you know.'

'Cath?'

'Yes?'

'Why don't you eat something?'

Most days, someone said, *why don't you eat*, as though I were making a choice to refuse food. Switching off hunger isn't purely volitional. What people don't understand is how scared I was, because I *couldn't eat*. I wanted to eat. I really did. But I genuinely believed that it was the wrong thing to do, and therefore that I would be punished if I did it. If I ate, I would go to Hell.

5. Easter

I sat alone on the far end of one of the pews, with the other Catechumens. After a series of scripture readings, we were presented to the parish community, who prayed for us with the Litany of the Saints. Next, the priest blessed the water. We renounced our sins and professed our faith, after which we were anointed, sealing the covenant created in baptism. Once all the Catechumens had been blessed, we were invited to take communion.

I knelt and bowed my head in humility and modesty while I took the bread and wine. It was an act of sacred cannibalism, in symbolic form, I was eating Jesus, becoming Jesus, the tasting was literal, I ate the end of shame, the end of guilt, I ate Grace. I understood quite literally that Christ died to save me – by providing bread I had earned during months of hunger hell.

I returned to my room. I had planned to break my fast with a hot cross bun, since not only is bread the body of Christ, but also I had not eaten carbohydrates for months. Folklore said that a piece of it was given to someone who was ill to help him or her recover. I went to my room and looked at the bun and picked it up and ground it into dust and placed it in the bin.

I was just about sensible and rational enough to know in body and mind I was ill, but I had so many restrictions and limitations in place, so many laws and so many precise habits. My System was ultimate, and challenging it would lead to Doom. I had no idea how to exit. I knew I had not reached the moment of return, but was only now beginning the process of descent. Steel cold fear gripped me and I felt I really might die.

6. Trinity

Most anorexic women wait mutely all their lives rather than profane the purity of a page with anything less than what is perfect. Texts I produced in the throes of the illness, such as my dissertation, *On Grace and Will*; *Swan Song*, the bildungsroman I wrote in 2012, and my diaries, are typically opaque, apparently schizophrenic: they contain pronouns, impersonal sentences, torrents of undigested quotations, which make a patchwork quilt, impenetrable as a *palimpsest* and confusing for the reader. I turned to a splintered or fragmented form of composition, and produced work more on the side of 'figuration' than 'representation'. Anorexic text is similar to the anorexic woman, in that it undertakes the torturous task of saying something without speaking.

Clarissa, or, the History of a Young Lady by Samuel Richardson, is regarded as the longest novel in the English language (*Hamlet* is the longest play). The heroine starves herself to death in penance for – or, perhaps, revenge against – her rape. The novel uses a strange excess of words in contrast to the savage reduction of Clarissa's flesh, as if the body of the starver is devoured by an internal verbosity. Words, strange and vampiric, feed on flesh. In recent decades, a prominent strain of Richardson criticism has been the argument that the erotics of the text undermine the author's expressed intention to provide a heroine who is morally exemplary. Some critics go so far as to suggest that Clarissa is complicit in her own rape.

How different, then, was it to be raped by a suitor in 1747 than today? Violent partners still depend on the complicity of the society around them and the silence of their victims, who fade into anorexic Christian martyrdom, as Clarissa does. I have nothing but admiration for the way Richardson depicts her efforts at recovery: centuries before talk therapy and trauma theory, Clarissa goes over the event again and again, in letters and in reported conversations, remembering, meditating, and praying over it, accounting for what she might blame herself for and what she suffered undeservingly.

Unlike other kinds of addictions, anorexia disguises itself as virtue. It felt good to deny my appetites and suppress my hungers, to excise them, or cause them to not be, which is another way of saying

I had begun to feel that desire was inherently wrong. I felt it was bad to allow things to penetrate my body, and flesh was proof of having done so in the past, proof of my previous 'sins'. By denying my desires I was able to erase them, which was a way of conquering myself. I wanted to create a pure, empty and static inner space, free from contamination or intrusion. I felt that my body was 'sullied', and wished it would 'melt' (The first line of Hamlet's first soliloquy, 'O, that this too too solid flesh would melt' is hotly debated among editors and scholars. The First Folio reads 'solid,' but the early quartos read 'sallied', a variant of 'sullied.' I favour the later.)

In a book called *On Shakespeare and Christian Doctrine*, I had come across mystic and philosopher, Simone Weil. She says that 'at the centre of the human heart, is the longing for an absolute good' and to achieve this, she demands a continual 'self-erasure' and 'detachment' from the 'ego'. My path had in common with Weil's a 'self-effacement' or 'de-creation', to use her terms. I became fascinated by her perilous emphasis on self-renunciation, her struggle to formulate a 'rhetoric of faith' of terrifying severity: my greatest desire was to become self-less, 'to lose all personal being' which is the condition Weil says is necessary to experience and know 'truth'.

Eating disorders have inspired a perverse literary tradition – an *ecriture faminine* – replete with patron saints (Catherine of Siena, Simone Weil), glamorous elders (Emily Dickinson, Jean Rhys), tropes (fairies, snow), and devices (paradox, irony, the unreliable narrator). In 'How to Disappear Completely: On Modern Anorexia', Kelsey Osgood argues that 'the person writing about her own struggle fuels the fire by producing a long, hubristic poem, an elegy, an ode' to the illness. She thinks 'we make anorexia desirable by connecting it to brilliants and also by talking about it poetically, by making it something that enhances a person's aura, makes them more glamorous.' I do not agree. I think that by committing the self-mythologising qualities of their sickness to paper, 'recovering' anorectics are trying, in their way, to express an entire system of metaphysical belief.

In the depths of my illness, I didn't regard myself as a fragile poet-fairy or believe I could paint with all the colours of the wind. I didn't imagine I could subsist on the minerals from the air, like an orchid. I looked death in the face, and by death, I mean death as we live it today, without God, without hope of salvation.

7. Hong Kong

Once I had submitted my dissertation – a minor miracle – I returned home to Hong Kong and, within a few weeks, my BMI had dropped again. I had begun to invent new ways to occupy my fanatic interest in numbers and orders and systems in order to 'prove' the existence of the soul. What follows is an example of the blatant nonsense, which composes my diary entries from that time:

> *E=MC2. 'c' is the speed of light, 'm' is the mass of anything, 'E' is the equivalent energy of that mass. This equation means that mass acts in accordance to the forces of light, to become energy, movement, action, 'life'. My mass is 46kg, but I'll round it to 50.*
>
> *According to Einstein's equation, I am a bundle of energy equivalent to –*
>
> $E = mc^2$
>
> $= m \times c \times c$

$= 50\ \text{kg} \times 300000\text{m/s}^2 \times 300000\text{m/s}^2$

=4,500,000,000,000 Joules!! That's 1.07552581 × 10^{12} calories!

With this energy, I could supply electricity for the entire world for days! If the average man burned 2,000 calories a day, I have enough energy for 18416 human lives of 80 years each! The Buddhists were onto something! In a sense, I have more than one life. But human beings don't have enough technology to convert ourselves into pure energy.

If it were possible to convert matter fully into energy then I could calculate the total annual energy requirement of human kind. In 2005 the Earth's total energy use was 5×10^{20}J. m=E/c^2 so m=$5\times10^{20}/9\times10^{16}$ = 5500kg – just 5.5 tonnes of matter. But matter cannot be converted into energy without the inclusion of light – 'c' – this backfires. It will not be removed from the life possessing it. Some people argue that it weighs 21g. Not so. Light, like 'qi' and spirit, is massless, but I nevertheless operate in accordance to it.

One day, when I was out running, I fainted.

I didn't 'See the Light'. I had the opposite experience.

I was teleported to Hell, where Harpies escorted me into a cell. I saw a group of young people within and blurted out, 'Oh, we must be the suicides!' but no matter how much I tried, I couldn't elicit a response from any of the damned souls around me. The cell had snakes all over the ground. They threw me against the walls and pierced my flesh with their claws. My flesh was eaten right to the bone, only to immediately grow back so they could eat it again.

Hell was not red and noisy. Hell was an absence of sense, there were no screams or sounds, Hell was not populated, it was only 'I' and the 'I' that thinks and not the Eye that sees. Burning there was, but it was not fire or ice burning or anything of flame or water, it was only self-burning, just a self, the self, burning for and on its self, fuelled on and by and for its self, self-consumed and so becoming less and less as it burns more and more inwards releasing the chemical composition of its heart into its bloodstream and evaporating it.

Three minutes later, I woke up.

That is my happy ending. I woke up.

Yes, Hamlet does appear as a Christ-figure in the final scene, because he dies and through his suffering, the soul (of Denmark) is saved. The New Testament's story is not, to put it mildly; the only one humanity has ever come up with about a Dying God. Transcendent power goes down to the dark and allows itself to be extinguished but then returns all the stronger. Selves, like stars, are entitled to eclipse. You get the happy ending *because* of the tragic one.

The psychologist William James (1842–1910) draws a contrast between two different kinds of people, the 'once-born' and the 'twice-born'. He says that the twice-born war with their flesh and live one long drama, and that, in a desire to understand the meaning of life, this attitude inevitably leads to a psychopathic crisis. He says that the process of unification, while gradual, can and does occur, and it transforms the most intolerable misery into the profoundest and most enduring happiness. But that's another story.

Anorexia is not a trivial concern. Anorexia is a fatal disease that has the highest death rate of all psychiatric illnesses. It may be a gross misunderstanding of Neo-Platonism, or an unusually disastrous variant of Cartesian dualism, but anorexia is not just a relentless pursuit of thinness. What am I really? What is the substance that stands the change and is the actually existing thing? There is something more eschatological at stake in self-starvation than the fashionable taste for slenderness or the equally fashionable ideology of self-control. Striving to be thin conceals the ideal not to have a body, which is not a trivial concern. Anorexia is a search for an 'I' that is anterior to name; gender; action; fashion; matter itself.

It is important to recognise that those suffering from eating disorders often carry the added burden of stigmatising attitudes from the lay public and the medical profession. Eating disorders and their sufferers are commonly looked down upon as being preoccupied with superficial issues. In fact, anorexia can be a complex way of managing existential and spiritual crises. The theoretical contributions of philosophy and theology can help treat and encourage today's sufferers. Abnormal eating is not just a psycho-pathological phenomenon, but the coherent implementation of moral values with a long tradition in Western culture. Contrary to theorists who analyse the desire for thinness primarily as a response to contemporary popular culture, thinness does not have much to do with what we believe to be nice or beautiful – it is not simply a matter of what we find *pretty*. It is a matter of what we believe to be *good* and *right*. Eating disorders are not just the symptoms of an underlying mental disorder, as is often argued. They are the symptoms of extraordinary morality, which is being taken seriously – or more seriously than usual.

Epilogue

1. Hong Kong, 2015

"Was it suicide?"

A friend of mine, whose brother died from complications associated with anorexia nervosa, confronted me with this question one night in an alleyway where I stood smoking outside a bar. Her eyes were black with anger and wet with sorrow. I felt chastened like a porcelain angel overlooking Armageddon.

She had spent the evening watching me chew ice while others ate food and drank wine. She knew I had nearly died, that I was ostensibly recovering but still 'practising', and she posed the question rhetorically, to create dramatic effect and make a point. I stubbed out my cigarette, said, "Goodnight", and we parted.

I returned to my apartment, opened my laptop, and, in a single, nicotine-fuelled fit, between midnight and sunrise, years after the events it records, I wrote *My Oxford*.

Our motives are rarely pure and never simple.

I wanted to help my friend, others suffering, and those supporting them, but – more urgently – I wanted to justify or maybe apologise for an experience that tormented me still, to provide an account of myself as a person of rectitude and righteousness. During the course of my illness, many people cast aspersions on my character. The disparaging, critical remarks (and looks) I received made me feel like a moral monster, courting death and wreaking havoc on all those who loved me.

It would have been easy to interpret my behaviour as a vanity project – I was an aspiring actress and model, an ambition which, in the years immediately following my graduation from Oxford, I pursued in London to its inevitable conclusion: boredom and poverty. I kept my religious conversion to myself, for reasons obscure to me now.

I settled in Hong Kong to establish a writing career while working as an English teacher. At first, I hated it. I hated the crowds, skyscrapers, sewers, humidity, and sunsets of whatever colour. I hated the expatriates who paused in their debauchery only to belch aphorisms and olive pips. I hated the furious gods with green faces and red eyes. Everything was moist and smelled like fermented fish or joss sticks, mung bean cake, oil, duck-mess and gasoline. I always felt contaminated, like the pollution was sinking into my skin, dying my blood black. But help was there, and slowly, over time, I got clean. I learned to receive food, process it for nutrients, and expel waste. I learned to accept experience, integrate its meaning, and eliminate toxins. In other words, I learned to write.

Of course, writing is not always helpful for everyone. I must be careful not to overstate my belief in Art. The "risk", the artist's existential dilemma – "give me genius or death" – is the same for the anorexic. The ballerina puts on the enchanted shoes, which transform her into a great dancer. The price is that she cannot stop. It is the nature of a person's writing that is key to its effects. When I was anorexic, I was parsimonious with language. As my eating disorder metamorphosised, I produced a whole anthology – hundreds of thousands of words: plays, diaries, letters, essays, novels. Reading them now, I am dizzied by the somersaults of energy. I purged, cleansed, and purged again, and God, it was good – to let the bewildered, chaotic fragments pour out. It was the catharsis that prepared me to say in one small nugget what I had taken years to metabolise:

No, it wasn't suicide. It was salvation.

"Eve initiated this," writes Simone Weil of the human condition in *Waiting for God*: "If we lost our humanity by eating a fruit, the reverse attitude – looking at a fruit without eating it – must be what saves".

These days, I'm less inclined to take Weil literally. When she died, age thirty-four, the coroner pronounced it suicide. She may have been a paragon of virtue, and admiration for someone provokes imitation, but Weil's eating habits are difficult and dangerous to emulate. A life that ends in self-destruction is not a guide for our own. We can be duped by our saints.

We condemn Eve, but we can't one-up her. She plucked, she ate, and all was lost, as Milton puts it. Sometimes, we ache with nostalgia for the lost paradise: we raid nurseries and buy seeds, mulch and compost and reap and sow with our hands full of earth, coaxing life out of the dull, dry grass. Then, fire scorches the earth, and if we survive the crucible, we rise, uncertain of what fate awaits us when the smoke finally clears. It takes strength to remember; it takes another type of strength to forget.

In *The Emigrants*, W. G Sebald says that "memoirs are like one of those evil German fairy tales in which, once you are under their spell, you have to carry on to the finish, till your heart breaks, with whatever work you have begun – in this case, the remembering..."

We need forgetfulness as well as memory. I don't think phoenixes have to remember every stupid damned thing they've ever done for five billion years. Butterflies have no memory of being a caterpillar. It is said that the unicorns did not board Noah's Ark in time to be saved from the Great Flood. Perhaps some animals obeyed God's admonition not to eat from the Tree of the Knowledge of Good and Evil. But we didn't. We ate. That's what makes us human. I eat, therefore I am.

2. Ecbatana, 8th century BCE

But what of Clarissa Harlowe? What of others like her? What of Tess of the d'Urbervilles? What of Lucrece?

There are countless portraits of rape in literature, but contemporary focus on the subject pays them little heed, dismissing them as glamorised or mythological and, therefore, I assume, pertaining not at all to reality, morally useless.

The Book of Tobit tells the tale of Sarah and Tobias. Sarah is a maiden cursed by an evil demon named Asmodeus, who will kill anyone she marries on the wedding night. She has already lost seven husbands when, guided and aided by the angel Raphael, Tobias finds her, marries her, and exorcises the demon (by burning the heart and liver of a fish – go figure).

There is an abundance of exegesis of this story, typically covering its parallels with Job, its significance as an intertestamental text and its canonical status. Luther describes it as a "delightful, devout comedy" that resolves, as comedies often do, in a happy marriage. Most interpretations cast Tobias as the hero: he acts bravely, stout-heartedly and chivalrously; he is helped by a divine figure; he risks his life; and he wins the maiden by defeating the monster. But, as Kierkegaard puts it in *Fear and Trembling*, "Any man who has not the courage for this is a mollycoddle who does not know what love is, or what it is to be a man, or what is worth living for".

There is little discussion of how and why Asmodeus began afflicting this particular girl in the first place. Why did the demon appear to her, and under what circumstances? Did Sarah summon him, or did he inflict himself upon her?

Sarah's tragedy is that she was deprived of the ability to give herself in love. This is an infinitely greater cause for grief than the sorrow of a young girl who has not yet found love. But – and this is her redemption – she is willing to be healed. She is the true heroine because of her ability to accept love even though she is fallen.

It is simply the case that the possibility of sexual assault or abuse must be assessed, and the results included, in any comprehensive therapy plan for eating disorder patients. Emaciation is listed among the symptoms of lovesickness in ancient and medieval physician's handbooks. Treatment includes laxatives, phlebotomy, exposure to light, gardens, and warm baths filled with water lilies and violets. I approve of all that – even the bloodletting, which relieves amenorrhea. But the best and most highly recommended cure for a broken heart is to acquire a lover. Even God needs love. Perhaps that is why he created us. He desired love so much, and a great desire for love can call love into being.

3. Sydney, 2017

When I fell in love, I fell from a very great height, from where I soared – high in the quiet, clear space where maths and poetry reside – through the time and space and stars and sky, grabbing at clouds, into the arms of a man who set my feet upon this rock and made my footsteps firm.

We'd loved one another before. We met at the dawn of our lives, before Hong Kong, before Oxford, before Ecbatana, in the Golden Age when androgynes roamed the earth. We were wild and unruly and threatened to scale the heavens, so the Gods cursed us by splitting us in half. We spent our dark ages groping to return to one another, and once we found each other again, the curse was lifted. It was my homecoming. I returned to Australia, my birthplace, and married him.

4. Sydney, 2024

While I was pregnant, I had a conversation with a woman so convinced that she would die giving birth that she decided not to have children. I told her the reason I want children: I believe, despite some evidence to the contrary, that existence itself is intrinsically good: it's better to be than not to be. That is, it is better to exist than not exist.

The "To be" speech demonstrates the enormity of what the human mind can contemplate and achieve and invites us to participate with Hamlet in exercising and appreciating its power. Indeed, the mind is at the centre of the play: the main interpretative question is whether or not Hamlet has lost it.

The body, on the other hand, is, to put it mildly, a problem. *Hamlet* gives us an anatomical catalogue: we hear of eyes, ears, heads, hands, faces, tongues, the skin, hair in general, beards, limbs in general, arms, legs, feet, toes, fingers, the thumb, the breast ("bosom"), the mammary organ (Osric's "dug"), genitals in general ("privates"), male genitals ("cock" and the "long purple" flowers whose common name has been euphemised to "dead men's fingers"), female genitals ("country matters"), and the anus ("bunghole"), hearts and brains, the lung, stomach, spleen, liver, guts, bones, marrow, nerves, sinews, spinal cord, arteries, blood, tears, sweat, milk, fat, gall, moles, cankers, warts, ulcers, and "contagious blastments." The stage becomes a veritable dissecting room, and, at the end, there are at least six dead bodies on display, not including Ophelia's.

Hamlet expresses utter contempt for the body, which serves only to deform human beings and ultimately reduce them to nothing. The body is, in short, the source of suffering, sin and, ultimately, death.

I almost died during childbirth. I lost 2.5 litres of blood in a postpartum haemorrhage, which was caused by a retained placenta. After my obstetrician tried and failed a manual removal – during which I felt pain and horror on another dimension to that caused by labour or delivery – a surgeon used a suction device to perform an extraction. In the following days, I received three blood transfusions. A woman in Australia with a similar birth experience would have died in 1950. The retained placenta complicates 0.1% of pregnancies but still has a fatality rate of 10% in the developing world, resulting in around 70,000 maternal deaths annually.

Philosophers have always asked whether it is bad to die, whether immortality would be good, how one might die well, whether there is life after death and what it might be like, and much more besides. The very first lesson of philosophy is that all men are mortal. And Socrates is a man; therefore, Socrates is mortal. We are mortal creatures who wrestle with our mortality and engage in soliloquies and syllogisms, forms of reasoning in which conclusions are drawn from given propositions. We love talking about rationality and death, which makes us seem serious and smart and reconciles us to our own extinction.

But Socrates was also born. He, too, was conceived, gestated in the womb, and then delivered from it. In fact, all men are born, but afterwards, this premise recedes from even the mother's memory to inhabit a chthonic under realm where fertility goddesses constellate to read diet books and tarot cards and assume sex positions from the Kama Sutra. Few claim to remember being born, but amnesia does not confer license to repudiate our origins. No one remembers being dead, and that doesn't stop us from formulating accounts of our humanity.

The increasingly popular messaging of the

natural childbirth movement promotes ideals about birth being orgasmic or ecstatic. That is exclusive, uncommon, and, for many, unobtainable – but I, personally, did have an experience for which the only appropriate adjective is mystical.

During the second stage of labour – the time which spans from when the cervix is fully dilated to when the baby is born – I had an experience I explain through the analogue of the eye. The word "autoscopy" ("self-seeing") usually describes "out of body" experiences, a phenomenon in which a person perceives the world as if from a location outside their physical body. I had an autoscopic "in-body" experience: I saw inside my own body. I saw with my internal organs, nerves and tissues my son pass through the birth canal, pelvic bones, vaginal opening, and descend into the world. This "inner vision" gave me an ineffable grasp of a reality that involved unity, "one-ness", with an infinitely perfect creator.

To some, this sounds like utter nonsense, woo-woo in the extreme. Indeed, *Imago Dei* – the idea that man is like God – could give rise to any number of misunderstandings, including that deification leads to blasphemous self-aggrandisement. If that were the case, then mysticism would be the most sublime, spiritualised form of egoism. *Imago Dei* is, in fact, an act of self-recognition in which the viewer takes itself as its own object of understanding, discovers itself as the image of God, turns toward the divine Archetype and enjoys personal communion with Him.

The body I once thought had to be de-created became the site of creation and showed its goodness by bringing forth what is good: a child. Creating does not just give us catharsis but is also a participation in God insofar as it brings something good into the world. Having a child and writing *My Oxford* are both good things, and it's good that they exist. We are not just "living towards death" as Heidegger says, and not just recollecting the past, but also creating and redeeming the future.

The author of *My Oxford* displays total disregard for her future, which she writes off as "another story." Fair enough. Happily Ever After is almost impossible to depict. Even Dante acknowledges the difficulty. You have to wish upon a star, want the fairytale, believe in love, go down to the fourth ring of the ninth circle of hell, spend however much time in purgatory, sit down, write "once upon a time", and hundreds of thousands of other words before you get to wings, halos, robes, harps, pearly gates, and the love that moves the sun and the other stars.

5. Sydney, 2025

The terror inspired by the doctrine of hell when you believe it exists and you risk going there is indescribable. It is a belief I acquired in Oxford. Recourse to the imagery of hell is remarkably common in the literature of Shakespeare's period: the majority of Englishmen and women worried about their own intermediate position on a vertical axis of salvation/damnation. At the final analysis, the "To be" speech isn't just about being or existence. It's about the "dread of something after death/ the undiscovere'd country": hell.

Eve's story and its Judeo-Christian heritage are critically important for the entire human race because it is intimately associated with alienation from God. Simone Weil admired Catharism – a word that, like my own name, comes from the Greek term for "pure". This medieval heresy held that the creation of humankind was a disaster and that spiritual purity, essential for salvation, would only be achieved for a scant few, through the strictest self-denial and starvation: only the utterly pure shall be saved.

There is another genealogy, which says we shall all be saved. David Bentley Hart, the contemporary evangelist for universal salvation, believes that "the idea of a hell of eternal torment to be unscriptural, logically incoherent, depraved, psychologically destructive, and morally corrosive". Heaven, on the other hand, he believes in wholeheartedly. There is an exquisite Greek word that appears only once in the whole of the Bible: *apokatastasis* (Acts 3.21). It means the "restoration of all things". Hart, and a line of others stretching back to some of the greatest church fathers, argues that such a restoration would include saving animals, the created world, and even Satan.

The relationship between religious asceticism and anorexia remains an obscure research topic, even though voluntary abstinence from food is a prescribed penitential ritual in most religious traditions. As William James writes in *The Varieties of Religious Experience*, "asceticism symbolises the belief that there is an element of real wrongness in this world, which must be squarely met and overcome by an appeal to the soul's heroic resources, and neutralised and cleansed away by suffering".

Ascetic self-denial is a curious phenomenon. It

is incomprehensible to a large number of people. As Nietzsche tells us, the ascetic strategy interprets sufferings as punishment, thus linking it to guilt. Every sufferer seeks the cause of her suffering. Someone is to blame; if you yourself are this someone, asceticism is a warranted response.

It is presumptuous of us to claim we know the eschatological state. We don't have a God's-eye view, and we don't know the final destiny of the soul and mankind. Creativity, with its focus on beauty, can serve as an antidote by offering a way to affirm existence rather than deny it. In Book 18 of *The Iliad*, Homer shows us Achilles's shield, upon which the entire past and future history of the cosmos is depicted. The effect of the passage is to lift us out of the welter of killing in which we are immersed so that for a moment, the moment of art, we see and celebrate life from the Archimedean point. Being able to "see" life like this is necessary if we are to bear being in it for the rest of the time.

I wrote this epilogue *in media res* – in the midst of things (which is where all the best stories begin). But every life-writer knows that only future events can bring out the true meaning of past and present events. The past is a potent force, with which we must reconcile again and again. Sometimes, I look back at my Oxford year and ask, who am I that this should have happened to me? How blighted I was! But then I think about today, and I ask the same question. What am I that this should have happened to me? How lucky I am! To what do I owe this good change in fortune: the future, which was once a threat, is now a promise.

CW
Sydney, 2025

Acknowledgements and Thanks

I am grateful to Gwen Davies, to the sponsors and students at Aberystwyth University, and everyone at *New Welsh Review.* I have also received kind support and encouragement from my family. I would like especially to thank James Sweetman, Benjamin Schaper, Duncan Driver and Holly Mak for their thoughtful comments about my early drafts. The staff of the English Department at the Chinese International School, with whom I worked while I was writing, were all invaluable mentors, as was Dr Sing Lee. Finally, I'm deeply grateful to my fiance, Adam Wesselinoff, for everything he is and does, and for being part of a happy new beginning.

PARTHIAN A CARNIVAL OF VOICES

PARTHIAN A CARNIVAL OF VOICES

NEW WELSH RAREBYTE